THE LITTLE BOOKLET ON

BUSINESS DESIGN

Getting Started

JONAS ALTMAN - MONIKA HESTAD

BRANDVALLEY PUBLICATIONS

The Little Booklet on Business Design: Getting Started
2nd Edition 2019
1st Edition 2013

This book is part of the series 'The Little Booklet on...'
Published by Brand Valley Publications
© Brand Valley Design Ltd, London 2019
All rights reserved.

Layout: Marianne Hollum Lydersen
Illustrations: Silvia Rigoni

Brand Valley Design Ltd
34B York Way
London, N1 9AB
United Kingdom

Brand Valley AS
publications@brandvalley.uk
www.brandvalley.uk

ISBN 978-1-912220-04-5

CONTENTS

Business Design helps entrepreneurs and
business developers take the principles of
designers to turn their ideas into reality. The method
starts with your customers' needs, incorporating
your vision and learning from your own experiences.
By combining analysis and strategic thinking with
intuition and visualisation, you're better equipped to
create impactful business ventures.

FOREWORD

By Mo-Ling Chui

I'm so pleased to write the foreword to this new edition of *The Little Booklet on Business Design*, which condenses and crystallises a wealth of knowledge, practice and business experience into a handbook format.

Deceptively simply, Jonas and Monika are able to distil current business design thinking into a clear practical framework. Because this has evolved out of workshops and their own practices as educators, designers and business consultants, the concepts and stages presented are adaptable to many different contexts. This mighty little booklet is packed with invaluable advice and strategic thinking for those wanting to birth business ideas and those wanting to re-orient, grow and refine purpose.

Design and innovation have always been key business competencies, now more than ever, in a changing contemporary business environment where uncertainty, disruptive technologies and new revenue models are the new normal. The Design Value Index reported that design-driven companies have outperformed the S&P (stock market) Index by 219% over 10 years.[1]

However, you don't have to be a tech start-up to be agile, prototype, validate and test. The Business Design framework can be effectively applied to lemonade stands, home brands, services or digital products. The tools and process set forward in this booklet provide sound guidance to balance entrepreneurial vision and motivation with shifting user market needs while developing a sustainable business model.

Most brilliantly, the booklet prompts readers to ask the right questions at the very right moments. Quoting Jocelyn K. Glei interpreting Business Guru Clayton Christensen: *'Questions are places in your mind where answers fit. Asking the right question invites expansion into a meaningful direction ....'*

The strategic questions posed in Business Design can help push your ideas forward from thought to planning and implementation in a practical way. Also the workshop outline, Helpdesk and tools are key resources and references to dig into.

The Little Booklet on Business Design is a perfect primer for students of business management or design, as well as entrepreneurs and businesspeople looking to update and align to a contemporary innovation mindset. That mindset takes a curious, adaptive, iterative approach to problems, where creative solutions are seeds of great business ideas.

Dig in and enjoy!

Mo-Ling Chui,

Course Director, BA (Hons) Design Management and Cultures London College of Communication, University of the Arts London

THE PROMISE BEHIND THE TITLE

Apply tried-and-tested design practices to help you launch your business.

As children, many of us opened our own lemonade stands. This business model relies on the same basic principles as any complex venture: how you make money (selling lemonade), what your cost structure is (buying lemonade) and how you develop your customer relationships (being friendly and endearing).

For some businesses, the lemonade model works well. For others, different ways of developing and bringing products to market have been employed. With technological advances, innovative businesses are re-engineering their business models all the time.

Today, a young entrepreneur may choose to give away her secret lemonade recipe in order to promote other products. Or she may deliver fresh lemons and other fine ingredients straight to her customer's door through an online subscription service. She could create a professional network, uniting young lemonade stand entrepreneurs on a platform to share experiences and support each another. The possibilities are, literally, endless.

As we witness an explosion in new businesses, there are companies that have failed completely, while others stagnate – losing market position to disruptors. Why are some businesses successful and others not? How do market leaders entice customers to spend their hard-earned money on products and services? What are the fundamental capabilities needed to succeed in a changing business landscape? Is it only our own creativity and drive that set the boundaries for our success, or are there other factors?

We believe that there are two essential ingredients for success. First, these new ventures put the experience and the values they would like to offer to the customer at the heart of their business. This in contrast to conventional businesses, which have focused their attention on the products or technology they are selling. Second, by doing so, they manage to attract and engage high-performing talent to their organisation. It's people who make the business, and it's their collective passion and effort that yield success. Such an enterprise not only turns a profit, but also provides a fulfilling sense of purpose for its workers. To help you develop such a resilient business, we encourage taking a design approach to the development of your venture.

Design has held a place in production for a long time. In the 1920s, design moved out of the guilds and into the factories. Back then, the mission for designers was to develop beautiful products that could leverage economies of scale.[2] In more recent times we've seen how corporations value the designer beyond her skill of making beautiful objects.[3] Where seats in the boardroom were once limited to financial executives or lawyers, progressive organisations now extend this invitation to designers. Others, like Airbnb, have co-founders who are designers by trade. And business schools have adopted design thinking when approaching the innovation process, which again changes the 'look and feel' and the content of books about business development.

Design as a discipline has broadened from being synonymous with product development and visual identity to include services, process and systems of work. It's a way of thinking that people without design degrees can engage with. It's this latter expansion that this booklet builds upon.

A company functions as a living system, much like the ocean. Waves are in constant flux as determined by the wind, tide, swell and seafloor. Organisations continuously evolve with people, technology, markets and structures. This is why the business design approach is a holistic one – helping you understand how all the moving parts might interact.

In fact, this is the same approach we took in developing this booklet. We derived insights through repeated testing in workshops with entrepreneurs and in real-world scenarios with clients. We've adapted the booklet over time through several iterations so you can now hold this current version in your hands. Design methods we build on in this booklet are playful and use visualisation to explore opportunities. These techniques allow you to look at a business challenge from the perspective of a designer. It places your potential customers at the centre of what you are developing and helps to clearly articulate the value you bring to their lives. In the tasks, we have also simplified the language of conventional business development to make it more intuitive.

At this early stage in launching your business, questions we invite you to consider are:

- Why are you starting this project or your business?
- Who are you creating your business for?
- Is there a real need for what you are developing?
- What are your values, and how do they inform the experiences you offer your customers and employees?

These questions may help you to stay focused on making things people actually want, instead of trying to make people want the things you make. These questions will also help you design a business you are proud to be a part of. By first identifying what inspires and drives you, you can create a culture that engages employees and an offering that draws customers.

Welcome to the world of Business Design, where your idea can be accelerated through a series of stages. And perhaps it may become the next big thing.

WHAT YOU WILL GET

The purpose of this booklet is to expose you to ways you can turn your idea into a viable business venture. The process of taking something new to market begins with the 'fuzzy front end',[4] because a new business concept may feel foggy and uncertain at first. You don't know which direction to go down or the first steps to take. The exercises in this booklet are designed to be hands-on to help you move out of the fog and into reality. The entrepreneurial journey starts with an idea. Before it's tested in the market, you'll learn that your initial idea does not need to be completely defined.

The four-step process introduced in this booklet – *Frame, Shape, Validate* and *Activate* – will help you crystallise your idea. In each of these stages, we present tasks that will help you to visualise your business and bring your ideas to life.

In the chapter on reflection, we will share five principles we have identified as crucial to developing a business: *Creativity, Resilience, Integration, Stability* and *Purpose (CRISP)*. Creativity is a driving force for any adaptable business. Resilience is required since building a business will have its ups and down. Integration of all of your activities towards the same goal is essential to keep alignment within your team. Stability is having a robust operation that you can then evolve over time. And finally, purpose is necessary, for without this, why are you setting up a business in the first instance?

Developing a business is a learning process. Every day you will gain a better understanding of what your business needs. In a fast-moving world, an emergent strategy helps deal with new demands and market shifts. And while planning plays an important part in any business, good execution is what really matters. During this developmental process, your original idea will evolve into something quite different. By the end, you will have an overview of Business Design and a methodology to help you build your venture.

Taking the time to explore our methodology will enable you to generate new and actionable ideas, to lead your team and advance your business. By dipping in and out of this booklet wherever you choose, you can:

- Develop a business concept that brings value to your customer.
- Be inspired to kick-start your business or transform your current venture.
- Define the reasons why you are in business and how you might better the world.
- Explore the benefits of good teamwork.
- Align your vision within a product and market context.
- Validate your business model.
- Profile prospective customers.
- Activate your plan.

A WORTHY IDEA

A business idea holds value when it proves an attractive proposition for a customer.

Before you begin our step-by-step process outlined in the next chapter, you need to have an idea that is worthwhile pursuing as a business venture. As entrepreneurs, we're constantly working with new ideas. Some are simply trifling thoughts that will quickly pass, while others take hold and grow. It is these latter ideas that we are interested in and for which this *Business Design* booklet was written.[5] You can find references to sources that can help you generate ideas in the Helpdesk at the end of this booklet.

WHERE DO GOOD IDEAS COME FROM?

There is no simple answer to this question. In this booklet, we have included four stories of how businesses may be born: *catering to customer needs, a happy accident, the marrying of two fields*, or *a result of patient persistence.*

The most ingenious ideas may emerge when you are relaxed, away from work, and idle. Funnily enough, you can get inspiration and gain epiphanies when you are not really thinking. Many will attest that their business idea came to them while on vacation or even in the shower. Some top entrepreneurs are known to take long walks or exercise regularly, while others keep a bedside notepad to jot down inspirations from their dreams. New ideas may also emerge when faced with hectic deadlines. There is also the possibility of developing a concept with others. Indeed, diversity drives innovation, and it's at the intersection of people, industries and disciplines where the magic really happens.[6]

Other important sources for new ideas are your potential customers. The main thing is to stay aware of when and how your ideas flow. Chance favours the prepared mind.[7]

Choosing the right idea to execute on is quite the challenge – the very best ideas may not seem all that promising at first. Only when a business idea is well established in the market, you will see if the business idea is viable. Our process will help with this and provide you with several tools to flesh out your idea and establish whether it's feasible. It's ideal for group workshops, allowing you to gain feedback and determine whether there is a suitable product/market fit. Sharing your idea may help you in this respect, but be aware that it's unlikely everyone will embrace your concept. Loving your idea is not the point, feedback is.

When inviting people to help you develop an idea, select those with diverse skill sets and make sure they complement each other. Everybody should be autonomous, aligned and solution-focused. Airbnb, the world leader in holiday rentals, was originally thought by many to be a bad idea. Paul Graham, the co-founder of the technology incubator Y Combinator, backed Airbnb, not because of the actual concept, but because of the passion and capabilities of the team behind it.

As your business develops, stay cognisant of your discipline, determination, flexibility and energy. All will play important roles. Your best ideas will align with your values and be something your team can galvanise around and build together. It doesn't hurt either if others have yet to pursue your business opportunity. This often means that there is a potential market for your idea. By adding your own personality and style in running a business, the idea may be considered unique.

THIS COMPANY WAS BORN OUT OF:
CATERING FOR NEED

In Sweden, a mandatory helmet law for children riding bikes led to a debate about whether the law should also be extended to include adults. Some opponents said they would rather risk injury than ruin their newly coiffed hair. Anna Haupt and Terese Altin took this as a business design challenge. They created a helmet that was 'invisible' until an accident occurred. At the moment of impact, a protective hood equipped with an airbag would instantaneously open. After seven years of tireless research and testing, they launched their product, and Hövding AB was born.

https://hovding.com

NEED AN IDEA?

If you are not already pursuing a business, here are some useful questions to ask yourself now. When you have answered these questions, suggest various solutions and you might have the beginning of a business idea.

'Is there something that annoys you, and likely thousands of others, every day? If so, can you envision a viable remedy for this annoyance?'

Answer:

Solution:

'Have you observed any unusual consumer behaviour that leads you to conclude there's a market opportunity just waiting to be seized?'

Answer:

Solution:

'How can your business idea contribute to a sustainable future?'

Example: The BRIGHT Product Company is one of many businesses aiming to address sustainable developmental challenges listed by the UN. The Norwegian company is committed to bringing light to those who don't have it. Their products allow millions all over the world to obtain light without access to an electrical grid. This means children can use BRIGHT solar lamps to complete homework at night and travellers can illuminate their path – increasing their comfort and safety.

UN Sustainability Goals:

1. *No Poverty*
2. *Zero Hunger*
3. *Good Health and Well-being*
4. *Quality Education*
5. *Gender Equality*
6. *Clean Water and Sanitation*
7. *Affordable and Clean Energy*
8. *Decent Work and Economic Growth*
9. *Industry, Innovation, and Infrastructure*
10. *Reducing Inequality*
11. *Sustainable Cities and Communities*
12. *Responsible Consumption and Production*
13. *Climate Action*
14. *Life Below Water*
15. *Life On Land*
16. *Peace, Justice, and Strong Institutions*
17. *Partnerships for the Goals*

'What can you do to solve the UN's Sustainability Goal no. ...?'

Answer:

Solution:

'How can you contribute to more ...?'

Answer:

Solution:

'How can you contribute to less ...?'

Answer:

Solution:

'Are there any imminent changes in the law that might create new business opportunities?'

Answer:

Solution:

'Have you had a life-changing experience? Many others have turned a negative event as well as a positive event into a fruitful business venture – could you?'

Answer:

Solution:

'What would happen if you combined your talent with that of a friend to create a complementary business?'

Answer:

Solution:

'Could you take your talents, expertise, and experience in one sector and apply them to another?'

Answer:

Solution:

Still have no ideas?

Take a bath, relax, and wait for that eureka moment. Or check out our resources and tools at page 103 for inspiration.

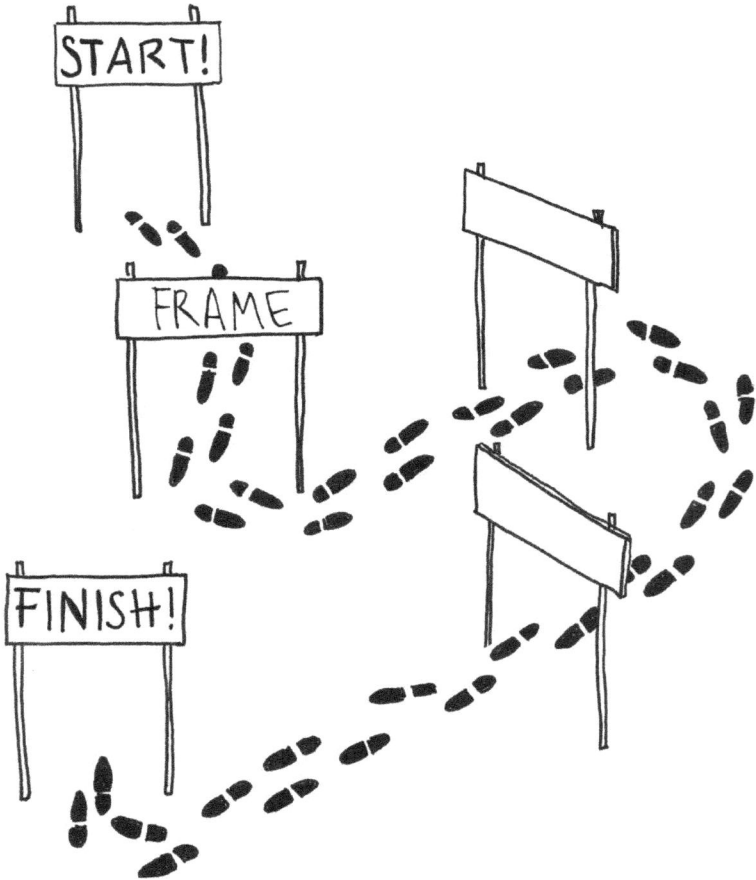

THE STEP-BY-STEP PROCESS

Provides a straightforward framework for developing your business idea.

The step-by-step process provides you with a natural progression for developing your business. You can approach these tasks in several ways:

As an exercise with pen and paper on your own
As a collaborative tabletop exercise with pen and paper
As a full workshop with visual aids

STAGE 1
FRAME

Turn your idea into a compelling business proposition that you can easily share with others.

TASK 1.1

ARTICULATE YOUR IDEA

Develop your idea by writing it down in full. Use as much space and do it as many times as you like until it makes good sense.

Define your idea by trimming it down to the two or three sentences. Remember to consider what you have to offer your customer.

Use the template on the next page to help you get started.

NOTE: The idea will develop as you start defining it. Revisit this task as you have progressed in sharpening your idea.

Loose thoughts and ideas:

Business idea:

How is it novel?

Who is it for?

What is your motivation for developing the idea further?

TASK 1.2

PROFILING YOUR CUSTOMER

Now it is time to identify who your customers will be and why they'll be interested in your idea. Will your business introduce a product for people to buy? Will you provide a service to individuals or to other businesses? Will you be selling a large volume of unique products in relatively small amounts or a smaller amount of popular items in large quantities – or both?

Draw up one or more profiles of your prospective customers. Focus on what their values, attitudes, behaviours and dislikes may be.

NOTE: If your business is providing a service or a product to other businesses, you can start with the profile of the businesses you are providing a service for.

Company

If your customer is a company, describe the organisation that will buy your service.

Organisation:

Decision maker(s):

Circumstances that make your proposal relevant:

Other topics:

End-user
Describe the person who needs your offering.

Name/profile:

Where they live, age and other facts:

Values that are important for this customer:

Circumstances that make your proposal relevant:

Other topics:

TASK 1.3

RESEARCH NEEDS

The intuition you used in profiling your customer goes hand in hand with your qualitative research. Specifically, which consumer needs do you intend to cater to in your business model? To reveal this, it's time to conduct research.

Make a sketch-model of your idea and share it with others. A sketch-model is a simple representation of your business. This could be simple sketches, a PowerPoint presentation or staging your business through a roleplay. The goal is sharing the idea with others in an easy way.

Plan how you can present your idea in a compelling way such that others can quickly understand it.

Introduce the sketch-model to as many people as possible. This can provide you with valuable feedback as to whether there is a real need for your business, and if so, how you can develop it further.

Which part(s) of the concept would you like to test (first sketch)?

NOTE: When conducting this kind of research, be aware that a sketch-model does not give the same idea about your concept as if it was a fully functional model. If you ask the wrong people, you will get reactions to your sketch-model that, although maybe positive, will not be helpful. It's crucial to get feedback from your intended audience and really understand how to incorporate their input into your future prototypes. And should you have a truly original idea, people may need time to get used to it before they see its value. People often dislike the unfamiliar. Sometimes they don't know what they need until you show them.

In the sketch-model of your business idea, what would you like to achieve?

What are your assumptions?

Who will you introduce your sketch-model to?

Questions I will ask:

TASK 1.4

VALUE PROPOSITION

Once you have received some feedback on your idea, it may be time to define your value proposition. Think carefully about what value you can offer your future customer. Why will your customer choose your product over the competition?

Define the specific values or benefits you will bring to your customer.

Customer experience:

NOTE: Benefits are what you can offer your customer. For example, if you're building a cloud-computing business, a functional benefit is how you help people store their files in a safe way. Emotional benefits are how customers can store files in a way that gives them peace of mind. The self-expressive benefit of such a product is that you make others look professional or environmentally conscious by being updated on new zero emission technology.

Functional benefits:

Emotional benefits:

Self-expressive benefits:

STAGE 2
SHAPE

Flesh out your idea, define your mission, resources and processes.

TASK 2.1

MISSION

Similar to a superhero, successful businesses have a strong mission. In addition, they have a vision that describes what kind of society they want to live in. Your mission can be something you want to help the customers to achieve, or something the organisation wants to accomplish.

A vision has different levels of abstraction. It can describe the reasons for doing something, it can be based on what the organisation wants, and it can also have a societal dimension.

A powerful mission is typically short and inspiring.

Use the tool on the next page to transform your business idea into a powerful mission and vision.

TIP: You can choose where to start in this model. Some will know for certain how to earn money, but the societal value can be less obvious in the beginning. For others, it may be the other way around. The business idea is clearly defined, but the vision for why they are doing this is abstract and diffuse. How abstract the vision is depends upon what inspires you and your team. The most important aspect of this task is to get a tool to help you to fulfil the business' strategic potential.

VISION

MISSION

LEVEL 3
Why we are doing this for society?

LEVEL 2
Why we are doing this for our customers?

LEVEL 1
Why we are doing this for our organisation?

OUR VALUES
What we stand for?

OUR PURPOSE
What we can help others with?

OUR BASIC BUSINESS IDEA
What kind of business and
how we want to earn money?

TASK 2.2

PEOPLE AND PARTNERS

Teaming up with the right people and identifying strategic partners will be crucial in moving your business forward.

Map out all of the different skills you need to run your business.

Define who these parties could be. Based on your core business idea, who will be essential to have on your team, and who can be your partners?

Plan how you might best approach them, and when.

Make a mind map of the resources needed.
Identify what kind of people you'll need to realise the potential in your business idea. Define those crucial to your business and those you'll collaborate with as partners.

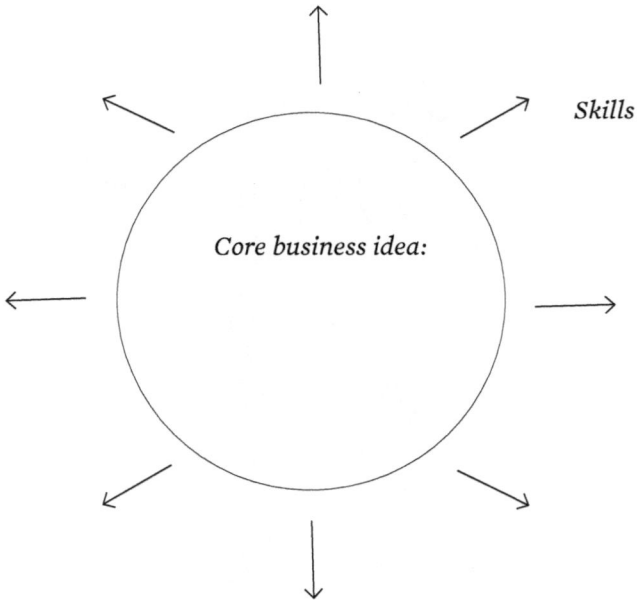

Skills

Core business idea:

How can you recruit the best of the best talent to help make your business idea a reality?

How can you build your network so it's aligned with your business idea?

What kind of leadership skills are necessary to execute your idea?

How will you get people aligned and committed to the mission of the company?

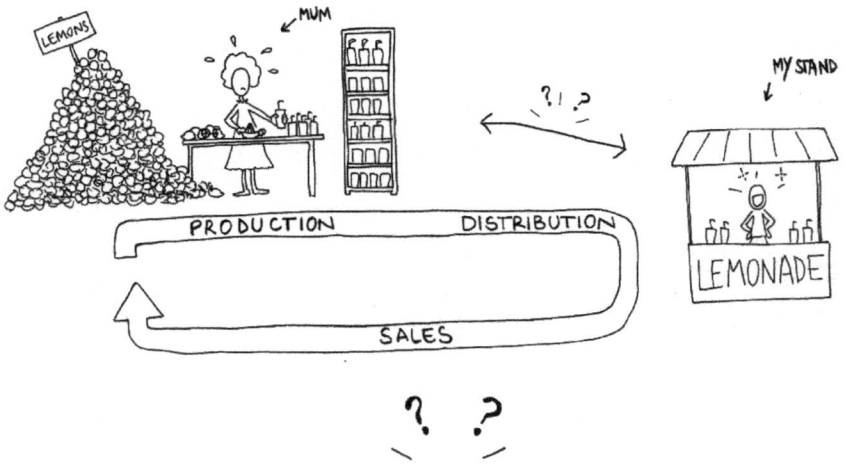

TASK 2.3

PLANNING AND PROCESSES

Every task in a company can be seen as a process: from developing your product and services to delivering your goods to the market to how you write a proposal to how you organise your meetings and so forth. What systems and processes do you require to make your idea a reality?

Visualise or write these down. Develop these processes by running various scenarios for your business. Ask yourself: 'What does selling mean to our business? How do we market our offerings? How much of the distribution are we in charge of?'

It helps to visualise what's required to develop your business concept – for example, a training programme for your employees, a routine competitor analysis, supplier guidelines, quality assurance or a customer relationship management system (CRM).

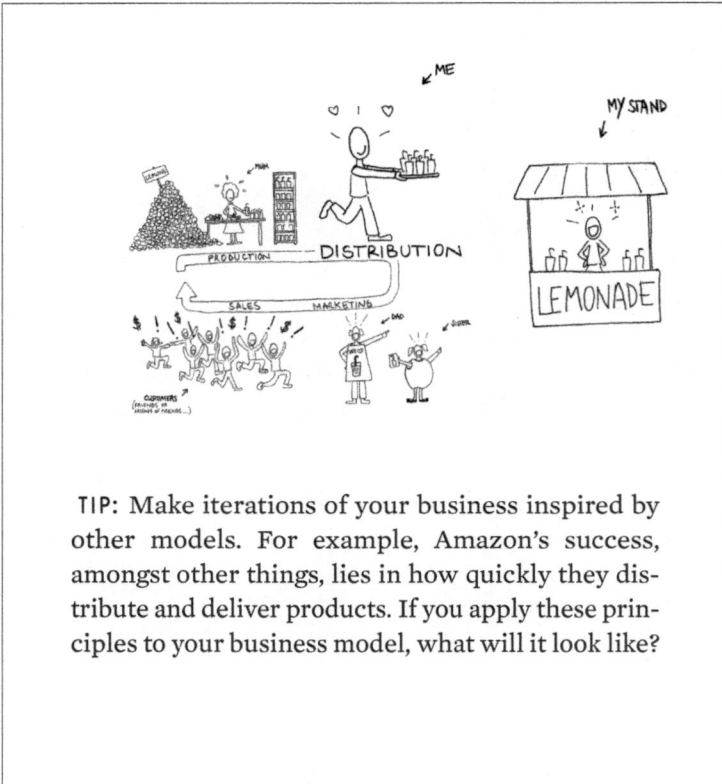

TIP: Make iterations of your business inspired by other models. For example, Amazon's success, amongst other things, lies in how quickly they distribute and deliver products. If you apply these principles to your business model, what will it look like?

Processes that make my business
Make simple visualisations and descriptions of the processes.

STAGE 3
VALIDATE

Assess your business's validity in relation to customer needs, potential revenue streams, earnings and expenses. Remember that start-ups often take a long time to be profitable and require greater resources than originally anticipated.

TASK 3.1

SWOT

Addressing opportunities and overcoming challenges are essential aspects of any entrepreneur's journey. They are part and parcel of developing and growing a business. In defining your business, conducting a SWOT (Strengths, Weaknesses, Opportunities, Threats) analysis is often useful.

Draw up a list of specific opportunities and challenges you may face. Be sure to communicate any assumptions you have made and the extent to which you will be relying on your team.

Invite others to discuss them with you. Have they raised other issues that you need to consider?

SWOT

Strengths:

Weaknesses:

Opportunities:

Threats:

TASK 3.2

MAKING MONEY

Now you know all of the key activities and what needs to be done. However, it's crucial you understand how to spend and make money.

Start by listing how you think you'll earn and spend money. You can do some research to find comparables and get an estimate on the numbers. This will act as a blueprint for your budget. You will continually update and amend this as necessary.

HOW WILL YOU EARN MONEY?
(Revenue stream)

For example, selling lemonade.
You can explore more than one revenue stream.

NOTE: The first year you set up your business, there's a good chance there will be a loss. You might therefore set out to break even in year two. Whichever way, your goal is to reduce expenditures and increase your revenue on an ongoing basis.

WHAT DO YOU NEED TO SPEND MONEY ON?
(Cost structure)

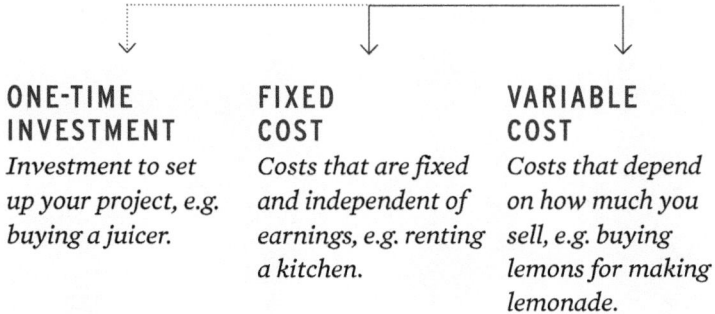

ONE-TIME INVESTMENT

Investment to set up your project, e.g. buying a juicer.

FIXED COST

Costs that are fixed and independent of earnings, e.g. renting a kitchen.

VARIABLE COST

Costs that depend on how much you sell, e.g. buying lemons for making lemonade.

What will it take for you to make a profit (earnings are higher than expenditure)?

TASK 3.3

BUSINESS MODEL

At the beginning of this booklet, we used a lemonade stand to explain a business model. Now it's time to define your own 'lemonade stand', whatever that might look like.

The illustrations show a traditional way to organise your lemonade stand. However, there are hundreds of other ways to organise your business. The emphasis could, for example, be on the marketing, on sales or distribution. Each will give you a completely different organisation and business model. In bringing all of these aspects of your business together, Alexander Osterwalder's Business Model Canvas is a useful tool.[8] This canvas displays all the key elements for building your business. When you have a clear idea for a business, this tool can help you quickly iterate on various business models. As you test your assumptions, continue to revise your canvas. Eventually, your own 'lemonade stand' will hold water.

Use the tool on the next page to combine all the basic elements of your business model.

> TIP: There are other similar templates on the market. If you want to explore a different template, you will find references to other tools in the Helpdesk.

The Business model canvas
Download this from https://www.strategyzer.com/
canvas/business-model-canvas

PARTNERS	KEY ACTIVITIES	VALUE PROPOSTION
the shop that delivers lemons (task 2.2)	*making and selling lemonade (task 2.3)*	*freshly squeezed lemonade delivered with a smile (task 1.4)*
	KEY RESOURCES *parents as an unpaid workforce (task 2.2 og 2.3)*	

COST STRUCTURE
lemons
(task 3.2)

> **TIP:** Many of the earlier tasks have touched upon different aspects of the business model. You can use these tasks actively when you compile the business model.

CUSTOMER RELATIONSHIP
direct sale by being charming
(task 2.3)

CUSTOMER SEGMENT
neighbours
(task 1.2)

CHANNELS
the lemonade stand (task 2.3)

REVENUE STREAM
lemonade sales
(task 3.2)

TASK 3.4

CONTEXTUALISE

All entrepreneurs have 'oops moments', but these can be mitigated if you've thoroughly mapped out your plan in advance. And more to the point, if and when things don't quite work out, you can learn from your mistakes.

Consider the wider context in terms of a PESTEL (Political, Economic, Social, Technological, Environmental and Legal) analysis.

PESTEL

PESTEL	Which trends or changes might affect you?
POLITICAL	
ECONOMIC	
SOCIAL	

TECHNOLOGICAL	
ENVIRONMENTAL	
LEGAL	

NOTE: In this task, identify those drivers of change that will be most important to your business.

STAGE 4
ACTIVATE

Find your motivation to take the leap.

TASK 4.1

SELF-AWARENESS

At the end of the day, starting a business and being an entrepreneur all come down to you – your own motivation and your persistence.

Define your own strategy of how you will take your business to the next level.[9]

PERSONAL STRATEGY

Where are you today?

What are you dreaming of? Where would you like to be?
Draw and describe your 'future you'.

How specifically will you get to 'future you'?

Who should you team up with?

What does success look like?

TASK 4.2

LAUNCH AND LEARN

Now that you have gone through the four stages and gained valuable insights, it may be time to launch your business.

Activate your business by curiosity and a wish to learn, and quickly seeing whether you're on the right track. You may very well find that the market responds in unexpected ways, that new opportunities have popped up or that your venture is developing much faster than you anticipated. Activation will help you validate your business model or indicate where it needs adjustment. You may also find that you'll want to start all over again from the beginning.

What are the three next steps you will undertake?

Step 1)

Step 2)

Step 3)

HUZZAH! Congratulations for completing the
business design process!

DIPLOMA

AWARDED TO

_____

For completion of a business design project

Project title:

_____

Date:

_____

THIS COMPANY WAS BORN OUT OF:
A HAPPY ACCIDENT

John Rowe, an avid hiker, was climbing mountains with friends in British Columbia, Canada. He had his precious jar of honey tucked away in his backpack. Rowe preferred natural honey products, as he came from a family with a rich agricultural tradition. This day, however, he tripped and smashed his jar. Camping out in bear country covered in honey, he feared he and his pals would not survive the night. Thankfully, they did. As a result of this mishap, Rowe spent the next ten years finding a way to convert pure honey into a solid form. His start-up, Honibe, was born, and has since gone on to win awards for the most innovative food business in Canada and the world.

https://honibe.com

THOUGHTS ON THE PROCESS

Step behind the scenes to see what makes up the four-stage process: *Frame, Validate, Shape* and *Activate*.

Our process is linear, but the development of any business is rarely so. Finding the time to pause and a step back will give you the opportunity to reflect and adjust your direction. Think of our process as cyclical, where you are just continuously improving.

The four stages – *Frame, Shape, Validate* and *Activate* – will not only assist in your planning, they will help identify the strengths and weaknesses in your business. Evaluating and re-evaluating your business with reference to these stages will help guide you in realising your goals.

Stage one: Frame
The inclination for humans to frame things is a simple and natural one. However, finding and framing the correct problem and the corresponding business solution can be complex.

Frame analysis can be traced back to the Canadian sociologist Erving Goffman, who was interested in the organisation of experience and the way we perceive the world. Like the picture frame that represents structure by containing its content, we similarly use a frame to hold our social experience. Understanding the needs your business caters to can be fleshed out by literally framing your offer – succinctly writing it down on a piece of paper. Getting your thoughts out of your head and into the world will help to clarify them.

All great ideas and the benefits they bring to this world begin with finding and framing the correct problem. Each business opportunity can be framed by answering a 'How can …?' question. In the Bronze Age we asked, 'How can there be a better and quicker way to move around?' – and the wheel was invented. In the twenty-first century, we asked, 'How can artificial intelligence enhance our memory, work and social lives?' – and Siri appeared.[10]

Framing a problem well brings the added benefit of inspiring and fuelling new and actionable solutions. While developing your business, periodically revisit this framing stage, as it's a helpful way to stay on track.

Seeking feedback is crucial in advancing your business idea. For many, this is a significant challenge to overcome. Don't be afraid to share your ideas with others – you may be surprised by how supportive or how insightful their suggestions can be.

Remember, the more radical your business concept, the more likely you will meet resistance. Ensure that you keep you biases in check, avoid over-selling your idea, and take on the feedback that counts. Seek out sceptics and be open to their suggestions – they will substantially help shape your future business.

Of course, there is a time to protect your business idea. Many entrepreneurs are overly fearful that their ideas may be copied. Remember that it is much harder than you think to execute well. Not everyone is ready and willing to undertake the investment required, so sharing an idea need not mean losing it. Furthermore, if you share your idea with people of integrity, it may prove to really benefit you.

If you suspect that your idea will be copied because there is some clear innovation in your process or product, then you may need to protect it.

Stage 2: Shape

In Business Design, *Shaping* is the stage where you bring your business proposition into focus. In this stage, you can make sense of all your research. After discovering your customers' needs and defining your value proposition, you can make wiser decisions about your future business.

Over the last two decades, research and development institutions, design firms and other consultancies have employed an array of tools, including qualitative research methods, business modelling, concept visualisation and open innovation. Additional tools can be found in our Helpdesk. These tools will be more effective and relevant if you place your customers' values and behaviours at the core. If you adopt an empathetic view of the world, your business will start to take shape as you reveal its true purpose.

During the *Shaping* stage, you should examine roles and scenarios. You as the leader, your staff, customers, partners and others play a particular role in relation to your operations. It's also useful to develop scenarios. Scenarios are what actually occur in your business, from clicking on the 'Buy Now' button on your website through to the shipping and invoicing of product to your customer. In this stage, we examine who and what makes your business tick.

Stage three: Validate

The *Validation* stage includes mapping out the business model, looking at opportunities for your business as well as the obstacles that might arise. Key considerations at this stage are how you're

THIS COMPANY WAS BORN OUT OF:
MARRIAGE

What if you took a technology company and combined it with a chocolate factory? This is what the co-founder of TCHO did when he married a Silicon Valley start-up with San Francisco food culture. Timothy Childs had previously worked on NASA's Space Shuttle programme, and his business partner, Karl Bittong, was a veteran of the chocolate industry. Merging Childs' drive for innovation with Bittong's passion for flavours was a match made in heaven. The company relies heavily on customer input as part of the development of its chocolate innovations. It has also designed a one-of-a-kind system for identifying and categorising specific chocolate tastes. Finally, it has championed a sustainable business model by empowering cocoa farmers and enabling the growth of local economies.

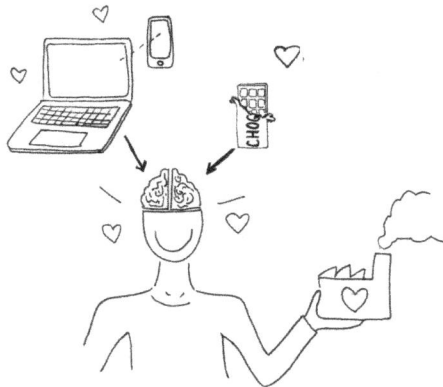

https://tcho.com

capitalising on the business prospects and your value proposition.

We have used the metaphor of the lemonade stand to represent your business. This simplified approach was adopted intentionally to assist you in visualising the various parts of your operation. It's unlikely that your business will fall squarely into the lemonade analogy. So when modelling your business, make sure to balance your intuition with pragmatism. SWOT and PESTEL analyses will help assess your business validity. But talking to customers is really the best way to gain confidence that you have a viable business.

In this *Validation* stage, you also stay aware of the context in which your business operates. As external factors are likely to impact your business, it is best to be adaptive so you can react quickly to changing circumstances. However, do not over-think this – developing a business, to a large extent, is about action.

Stage four: Activate

The final phase is the *Activation* stage, where you make it all happen. Here you see your initial idea emerge as a viable business venture.

A start-up is all about what the entrepreneur and the team manage to achieve together. If you are becoming an entrepreneur or getting a larger project started, you will have to make changes in your life. For example, it may be necessary to uproot your family and move to a new location. It's also likely you will need to arrange financing, whether from savings, family, friends, business angels, venture capitalists or banks. If you are launching a new project internally in an existing company, it must, for example, be anchored in the organisation, and you may have to acquire a budget and get resources. If the new business idea is radically different from the core business, you might have to start a new business to launch your idea. If you're ready to start, then it's time to activate and implement your strategy.

All of this may still seem like a long journey, but if you break the process down into bite-size pieces, it is much easier to get started. Go on – get ready to hang out your shingle and officially open your doors!

RUNNING THIS AS A WORKSHOP

This booklet can serve as a resource for individuals, but it can also be used to run a workshop. Each of the stages represents an important phase in the development of your business. The format of the workshop can be run over a single day or expanded to several days, allocating a whole day to each stage.

We invited designers, scientists, sales managers, technologists and entrepreneurs to help develop this booklet. Together, we explored the process, learned and improved the process. It helped some people to establish start-ups and others to accelerate their existing business. Each step represents an important stage in developing your business idea.

Have participants work in groups of four or five to develop a business concept. You can use completely fictional business ideas or real-life ventures.

Your workshop agenda could look like this:
- Welcome: An introduction to our process.
- Present the four 'born out of' stories to kick-start the brainstorming.
- Allow 20 minutes for each of the four stages.
- Remember to take breaks with refreshments where the participants can mingle, get information and get energised.

Workshop requirements
- large roll of paper
- A4 paper
- writing materials
- lemonade as refreshment

Some insights shared:

'The business design booklet's process allows people with fresh and more fully developed ideas to really push their business to the next level in a quick and practical way.'
– Rita Fernandez

'A fun and inspiring workshop that helps to develop your entrepreneurial skills.'
– Mariana Jungmann

THE BUSINESS DESIGNER'S HAT

Explore five key concepts vital to enduring entrepreneurship.

Behind our process are five important principles to help fuel you: *Creativity, Resilience, Integration, Sustainability* and *Purpose*. Integrating these into your daily work will help you master Business Design.

Creativity

Creativity is what will drive your business forward. Developing an idea for a business is just the beginning of a journey during which you must maintain motivation, and most importantly, be creative in both thinking and doing. Creativity is needed continuously: when coming up with your idea, when turning it into a viable business, when defining how to monetise, when implementing your marketing strategy and more. Most crucially, creativity is essential when fostering the right culture within your company. This, in turn, means that your team's collective creativity can flourish, granting a competitive advantage to your business.

Being creative in any field requires knowledge, enabling you to push the boundaries and develop something that is built to last. Running your business in today's marketplace will rely on your ongoing curiosity and insatiable desire to acquire new knowledge. It will rest on your cognitive abilities, integrated thinking, deep work and focus. By allowing yourself to gain and reflect upon new insights, you'll develop and enhance your creative skills. Constant trial and error, sometimes in playful ways, will be an important part of developing your business. Any successful entrepreneur can attest that some form of failure is inevitable – it's what you learn from it that counts.

Indeed, clever business leaders learn from problems, knowing that some setbacks cannot be avoided on the road to success. By discovering and accepting what went wrong and when, ascertaining why events happened as they did and how to avoid similar mistakes in the future, you can better achieve your goals.

Resilience

Successful entrepreneurs tend to be more resourceful and persistent than others. Creating a new market or revolutionising an outdated one involves taking enormous risks. Launching new and radical solutions in the market and successfully disrupting a market will require more tenacity and resilience than normal. It can be looked upon as driving against one-way traffic. If the founder is successful, there will be no competitors in the market.[11]

You will face sceptics in every area of your life. The strength to follow a lonely path and have confidence in your idea and yourself will be necessary before you can reap the rewards. Presenting your idea as a successful brand before you have a proper revenue stream is known as the 'fake it till you make it' approach in the fashion industry. This means that the business leader practises what social psychologists refer to as impression management.[12]

THIS COMPANY WAS BORN OUT OF:
PATIENT PERSISTENCE

In 1977, spurred on by the DIY aesthetic of the punk rock movement, a music fan decided to set up a record label to release music he loved. He promised himself that he would not prioritise money over creativity. When business was good and the label was thriving, he rejected several offers to buy his label. When business was bad and he was nearly bankrupt, he persevered. A blessing came in the guise of hit artists like Aphex Twin and Adele. His work ethic and belief in his business paid off. By keeping the promise he had made to himself, 40 years later Martin Mills is the CEO of Beggars Group, working out of his nondescript London office and loving every minute of it.

http://www.beggars.com

Building a new high-end fashion brand requires the designer to conceive and create clothes as well as produce an event to showcase the collection. The costs of materials and labour are expenses – but often the costlier one is the fashion show. In this crucial stage of the business, brand perception is everything. Behind successful high-end fashion brands, there is always a resilient entrepreneur.

After what may be years, and against all odds, you may feel you've made it. Rest assured, you will always need to be innovating. As new competitors emerge, being able to disrupt your own business can ensure you remain leader of the pack.

Integration

Integrating your operations with your core vision will help ensure that the moving parts of your business are optimised. This relies on effective leadership, worker engagement and strong collaboration, both within and outside your organisation.

The goal is to build an organisation that is responsive. The way you organise should suit your business such that the whole is greater than the sum of its parts. For example, the T-shirt company Threadless built a network of designers, artists, illustrators and anyone who loves T-shirts with a unique style. They encourage customers to vote for their favourite T-shirts as well as design new ones. Forming a resilient community around this shared love of quirky illustrated T-shirts, one-time customers can become artists as well as consumers.

Seeing your business departments as a system that works together will allow you to make small adjustments that have a big impact. By inspiring and engaging both employees and customers, you will create a progressive organisational strategy. This will contribute significantly to the success of your business.

Sustainability

It is certainly possible to do something that makes a social impact and money. In today's economy, more people than ever are striking the balance between purpose and profit. You need to be cautious, as your dream will not be enough on its own. Without a realistic way to sustain your business financially, there can be no longevity. Even non-profit ventures that often rely on public funding are finding innovative ways to independently sustain themselves.

It is a good idea to identify and exploit your revenue sources in your formative stages. Facebook first developed a platform enabling people to connect with each other, only later implementing a way to earn money from it.[13] The same applies to Amazon. Of course, this is not always possible, but it's worth appreciating that some companies today don't directly generate a profit from their principal business activity.

In many instances, planning for more than one source of income will help build a robust business infrastructure. Running lean means using the least amount of resources you need to expend in order to bring your initial product or service to market.[14]

First impressions are important, so doing your best to ensure your prototype is up to scratch will serve you well in the long run. Once you have delivered on your customer promise and are turning a profit, reinvest it wisely to help sustain your business.

Purpose

Having a sense of purpose for what you wish to accomplish, how you wish to spend your time and hope to direct your energy is a great place to begin for starting a business. It's easy for consumers today to survey the market and choose products or services of businesses whose values correlate most closely with their own.

Believing in something so enthusiastically that you actually develop a business out of it can be very rewarding, as both employees and customers are likely to adopt your vision. If your company is dedicated to exceeding customer expectations, it will excite such dedication among your customers that they will happily do most of the marketing and promotion for you.

Get out there, and good luck!

HELPDESK

Reference list, recommended additional resources and tools.

Business managers and design strategists are moving to a place where design meets business. Below are books that have inspired us when developing our process. We have included academic texts as well as inspiring books from practitioners. In the Toolkit section, you can find practical hands-on tools that can be used in combination with this booklet.

Business, creative and design mindset

Abbing, Eric Roscam. 2010. *Brand-driven Innovation*. London: AVA Publishing.

Belsky, Scott. 2010. *Making Ideas Happen: Overcoming the Obstacles between Vision and Reality*. London: Portfolio Penguin.

Brown, Tim. 2009. *Change by Design: How Design Thinking Transforms Organisations and Inspires Innovation*. New York: Collins Business.

Csikszentmihalyi, Mihaly. 2008. *Flow: The Psychology of Optimal Experience*. London: Harper Perennial.

De Bono, Edward. 1996. *Serious Creativity: Using the Power of*

Lateral Thinking to Create New Ideas. 3rd ed. London: Harper-Collins.

De Bono, Edward. 2010. *Lateral Thinking*. New ed. London: Viking.

Hestad, Monika and Rigoni, Silvia. 2013. *The Little Booklet on Design Thinking: An Introductory Workshop*. London: Brand Valley Publications.

Kelley, David M and Kelley, Tom. 2013. *Creative Confidence: Unleashing the Creative Potential within Us All*. London: Harper-Collins.

Kim, W. Chan and Mauborgne, Renée. 2015. *Blue Ocean Strategy: How to Create Uncontested Market Space and Make Competition Irrelevant*. Boston, MA: Harvard Business Press.

Lehrer, Jonah. 2012. *Imagine: How Creativity Works*. New York: Houghton Mifflin Harcourt.

Lewrick, Michael, Link, Patrick and Leifer, Larry. 2017. *The Design Thinking Playbook: Mindful Digital Transformation of Teams, Products, Services, Businesses and Ecosystems*. Hoboken, NJ: John Wiley & Sons Inc.

Martin, Roger. 2007. *The Opposable Mind: How Successful Leaders Win through Integrative Thinking*. Boston, MA: Harvard Business School Press.

Martin, Roger. 2009. *Design of Business: Why Design Thinking is the Next Competitive Advantage*. Boston, MA: Harvard Business Press.

Pink, Daniel H. 2008. *A Whole New Mind: Why Right-brainers Will Rule the Future*. London: Marshall Cavendish.

Pink, Daniel H. 2009. *Drive: The Surprising Truth about What Motivates Us*. New York: Riverhead Books.

Shirky, Clay. 2010. *Cognitive Surplus: Creativity and Generosity in a Connected Age*. London: Allen Lane.

Van Der Pijl, Patrick et al. 2017. *Design a Better Business: New Tools, Skills, and Mindset for Strategy and Innovation*. Hoboken, NJ: John Wiley & Sons.

Teamwork, innovation and organisational change
Altman, Jonas. 2020. *Shapers: Moving with the New World of Work*. London: Wiley (forthcoming).

Clatworthy, Simon. 2019. *The Experience-Centric Organization: How to Win Through Customer Experience*. Sebastopol, CA: O'Reilly Media.

Clear, James. 2018. *Atomic Habits: An Easy and Proven Way to Build Good Habits and Break Bad Ones*. London: Cornerstone.

Drucker, Peter F. 2008. *Managing Oneself.* Boston, MA: Harvard Business Review Press.

Drucker, Peter F. 1998. The Discipline of Innovation. *Harvard Business Review* 76(6): 149–57.

Edmondson, Amy. 2012. *Teaming: How Organisations Learn, Innovate, and Compete in the Knowledge Economy*. Hoboken, NJ: John Wiley & Sons.

Handy, B. Charles. 1991. *The Age of Unreason*. New ed. London: Random House Business Books.

Kotter, John P. 2012. *Leading Change, with a New Preface by the Author*. Boston, MA: Harvard Business Review Press.

McChrystal, General Stanley A., Silverman, David, Collins, Tantum and Fussell, Chris. 2015. *Team of Teams: New Rules of Engagement for a Complex World*. London: Penguin.

Shirky, Clay. 2009. *Here Comes Everybody: How Change Happens When People Come Together*. London: Penguin.

Tu, Khoi. 2012. *Superteams: The Secrets of Stellar Performance from Seven Legendary Teams*. London: Portfolio Penguin.

Von Hippel, Eric. 2005. *Democratizing Innovation*. Cambridge, MA: MIT Press.

Business modelling and entrepreneurship
Aulet, Bill. 2013. *Disciplined Entrepreneurship*. Hoboken, NJ: John Wiley & Sons.

Blank, Steven G. og Dorf, Bob. 2012. *The Startup Owner's Manual: The Step-by-Step Guide for Building a Great Company*. Pescadero, CA: K&S Ranch Press.

Godin, Seth. 2010. *Linchpin: Are You Indispensable? How to Drive Your Career and Create a Remarkable Future*. Kindle ed. London: Hachette Digital.

Osterwalder, Alexander and Pigneur, Yves. 2010. *Business Model Generation: A Handbook for Visionaries, Game Changers and*

Challengers. London: John Wiley & Sons.

Read, Stuart, Sarasvathy, Saras, Dew, Nick, Wiltbank, Robert and Ohlsson, Anne-Valérie. 2010. *Effectual Entrepreneurship*. London: Routledge.

Strategy
McKeown, Max. 2011. *The Strategy Book: How to Think and Act Strategically to Deliver Outstanding Results*. 1st ed. London: Financial Times/Prentice Hall.

Ries, Eric. 2011. *The Lean Startup: How Constant Innovation Creates Radically Successful Businesses*. London: Portfolio Penguin.

Rumelt, Richard P. 2011. *Good Strategy/Bad Strategy: The Difference and Why It Matters*. London: Profile Books.

Online resources and tools
Business Model Canvas:
https://www.strategyzer.com/canvas
Circular Design Guide: https://www.circulardesignguide.com
Design Management Institute: https://www.dmi.org
Ellen MacArthur Foundation: https://www.ellenmacarthurfoundation.org/circular-economy/what-is-the-circular-economy
Fast Company: https://www.fastcompany.com
Fast Company Co-Exist: https://www.fastcoexist.com
Forbes: https://www.forbes.com
Harvard Business Review: https://hbr.org
Inc.: https://www.inc.com
Investopedia: https://www.investopedia.com
Techcrunch: https://techcrunch.com
Ted Talks: https://www.ted.com/topics/entrepreneur
Startup Class: http://startupclass.samaltman.com

Startup Grind: https://medium.com/startup-grind
Strategy + Business: https://strategy-business.com
UN: https://www.un.org/sustainabledevelopment/sustainable-de-
velopment-goals/

Companies referenced in the text:
Airbnb: https://www.airbnb.com
Beggars Group: https://beggars.com
BRIGHT products: https://bright-products.com
Honibe: https://honibe.com
Hövding: https://hovding.com
TCHO: https://tcho.com
Threadless: https://www.threadless.com

ENDNOTES

1. Read more about the Design Value Index at: https://www. dmi.org/page/DesignValue/The-Value-of-Design-.htm.
2. Paulsson, Gregor. 1919. *Vackrare Vardagsvara*. Stockholm, Svenska Slöjdföreningen, Stockholm, Sweden.
3. There are several champions operating at the intersection of design and business. For example: Roger Martin (former Dean of Rotman School of Management), Rob Harvey (former Vice President of Herman Miller), Tim Brown (President of IDEO), John Maeda (President of Rhode Island School of Design) and David Kelley (Founder of IDEO and Creator of Stanford's d.school).
4. The concept of the 'fuzzy front end' was originated by Preston G. Smith and Donald G. Reinertsen.
5. If you need to develop an idea from scratch, our first booklet can help you with this: Hestad, Monika and Rigoni, Silvia. 2013. *The Little Booklet on Design Thinking: An Introductory Workshop*. London: Brand Valley Publications.
6. Johansson, Frans. 2004. *The Medici Effect: What Elephants and Epidemics Can Teach Us about Innovation*. Boston, MA: Harvard Business School Press.
7. Johnson, Steven. 2011. *Where Good Ideas Come From*. New York: Penguin Putnam.
8. Alexander Osterwalder's Business Model Canvas can be downloaded from: https://www.strategyzer.com/canvas (accessed 17 October 2019).
9. Inspired by Max McKeown. 2011. *The Strategy Book: How to Think and Act Strategically to Deliver Outstanding Results*. 1st ed. London: Financial Times/Prentice Hall.
10. From Ted Gruber's Ted Talk 'How AI can enhance our memory, work and social lives', which you can see here: https://www.ted.com/talks/tom_gruber_how_ai_can_enhance_our_memory_work_and_social_lives/up-next (accessed 27 September 2019).

11. The concept of the 'blue ocean' was developed by W. Chan Kim and Renée Mauborgne. 2005. *Blue Ocean Strategy: How to Create Uncontested Market Space and Make Competition Irrelevant.* Boston, MA: Harvard Business Press.

12. Bruder, Jessica. 'The Psychological Price of Entrepreneurship', *Inc 500 Magazine*, September 2013, p. 72.

13. Statistic from Henry Hitchings. 'From Town Criers to Trending Tweets', *Wall Street Journal*, 20 October 2013.

14. For example: Eric Ries. 2011. *The Lean Startup: How Constant Innovation Creates Radically Successful Businesses.* London: Portfolio Penguin; Steven G. Blank and Bob Dorf. 2012. *The Startup Owner's Manual: The Step-by-Step Guide for Building a Great Company.* Pescadero, CA: K&S Ranch Press.

AUTHORS

Jonas Altman - *author*
Jonas Altman is the founder of Social Fabric, an award-winning design practice with offices in London and Vancouver. Jonas creates learning experiences that empower leaders to transform how they organise and innovate. He has designed multiple fashion brands, launched a music agency, created London's first lifestyle and technology incubator, and worked with many of the world's leading organisations, including Google, Sony Music, the BBC, the Tate and Cancer Research UK. Jonas is an Adjunct Professor in Entrepreneurship and Innovation at UBC Sauder School of Business. He coaches entrepreneurs around the world about doing their best work, and writes for *Quartz at Work, Inc.com, Thrive Global* and *The Guardian.*

Dr. Monika Hestad - *author*
Monika Hestad is the founder of Brand Valley, an independent strategic consultancy, building on 15 years' research within design leadership and brand strategy. Monika has practised and lectured on design leadership and brand strategy since 2004. She teaches strategic design thinking in the MA Innovation Management at Central Saint Martins College of Arts and Design in London and design management at Oslo School of Architecture and Design in Norway. Monika is board member at the furniture company Helland Møbler AS. Her book *Branding and Product Design: An Integrated Perspective* is published by Routledge.

Monika has a Master's degree in Industrial Design and a PhD in Industrial Design and Branding from Oslo School of Architecture and Design.

Mo-Ling Chui - *guest contributor*
Mo-Ling Chui is Course Director for BA (Hons) Design Management and Cultures at London College of Communication, University of the Arts London. She is a creative director, strategist, curator and facilitator with almost 20 years' experience of developing, managing and delivering multifaceted projects internationally. As co-director of Current.works, she helps diverse organisations embed cultural research and build future-facing human-centred design competencies.

Silvia Rigoni - *illustrations*
Silvia Rigoni's background is a mix of product design, project management and innovation management. Her passion and field of speciality is food and health innovation. She has a BA in Industrial Design from Instituto Europeo di Design in Rome and a Master's degree in Innovation Management from Central Saint Martins, University of the Arts London. At present, she is working as an Innovation Manager at Cancer Research UK.

BRAND VALLEY PUBLICATIONS

Brand Valley's work is based on more than a decade of research in branding, design and innovation, with a continuous motivation to develop and share knowledge across these disciplines. The aim of the booklets is to enable and empower companies within the new economy. The philosophy behind these is a belief that people respond to businesses that are creative, integrated, value-centred, reflective and sustainable.

All of the booklets are collaborative projects between Brand Valley and partners in academia or other consultancies. Brand Valley Publications is the publication arm of Brand Valley Design Ltd (UK) and Brand Valley AS (Norway).

www.brandvalley.co.uk
publications@brandvalley.co.uk
Facebook: @BrandValley
Twitter: @brandval

ACKNOWLEDGEMENTS

The culmination of learning and inspiration for this booklet would not have been possible without the support of all the educators, colleagues, clients, family, friends and students along the way.

A special mention to our families, to Anders Grønli, Joel Altman and Trond Bjerge, for their patience and input.

Another special thanks to Komal Mangu, Ihna Stallemo and Anne Maria Røe, who while working at Brand Valley provided key insights that advanced our thinking. The students and colleagues at MA Innovation Management at Central Saint Martins, The Design Institute at Oslo School of Architecture and Design and Sauder School of Business also provided us with valuable insights at various stages in our process. We are also grateful to Huw Jones from Cove Publishing Support Services, who once again provided his efficient copy-editing services.

Your input and feedback improved the quality of the booklet as well as adding to the excitement of developing the process. We are looking forward to hearing about your ventures and furthering our thinking in collaboration with all of you.

www.ingramcontent.com/pod-product-compliance
Lightning Source LLC
Chambersburg PA
CBHW041217030426
42336CB00023B/3367